The Environmental Impact of AI Data Centers

Roggie Clark

Continue Learning At Our Website: Roggieclarkbooks.com

Continue exploring educational resources, tools, books, workbooks, and learning materials designed to help readers continue building knowledge and practical skills. Visit: www.roggieclarkbooks.com

Inside you'll find:

- Educational worksheets
- Beginner-friendly guides
- Printable activities
- Companion materials for books and courses

A growing library of educational content for readers, collectors, learners, parents, teachers, and lifelong students.

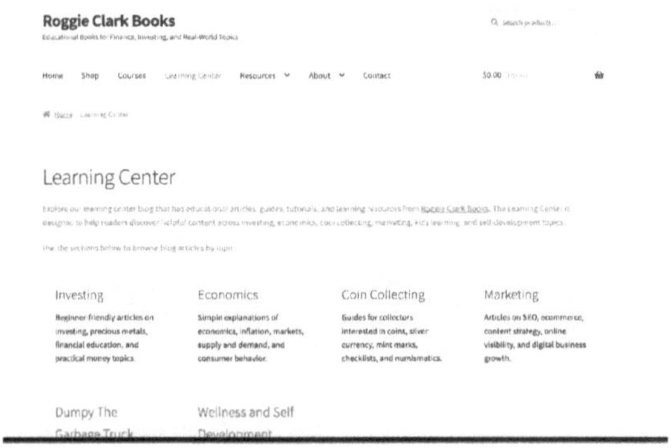

The Strategic Guide to U.S. Mint Gold and Silver Coin Investing

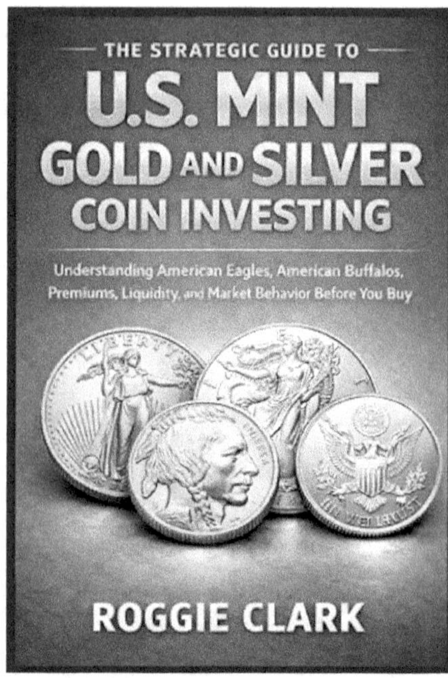

Rather than offering a general introduction to precious metals, this guide examines how American Gold Eagles, American Gold Buffalos, and Silver American Eagles behave in real investor markets.

https://www.amazon.com/Strategic-Guide-U-S-Silver-Investing/dp/B0GQKJF9K6

Copyright

Title: The Environmental Impact of AI Data Centers
Author: Roggie Clark

Cover Design: Roggie Clark
Editing: Renee' Clark

Printed in the United States of America

Disclaimer

The views and opinions expressed in this publication are those of the author and do not necessarily reflect the official policies, positions, opinions, or viewpoints of any individual, company, organization, institution, agency, or entity referenced or mentioned within this work.

The author is not necessarily affiliated with, endorsed by, sponsored by, or compensated by any individuals, companies, organizations, brands, institutions, products, or services referenced within this publication unless specifically stated otherwise. Any examples, sample situations, stories, illustrations, or scenarios presented may be fictionalized or simplified for educational purposes. Any resemblance to actual persons, living or dead, businesses, or events is purely coincidental unless otherwise stated.

The information, ideas, strategies, concepts, techniques, opinions, suggestions, and educational materials contained in this publication are provided on an "as is" basis without warranties of any kind, either express or implied. While every effort has been made to provide accurate and current information, neither the author nor the publisher makes any representations or warranties regarding the completeness, accuracy, reliability, suitability, or applicability of the information presented.

This publication is intended solely for educational and informational purposes and should not be interpreted as professional advice of any kind, including but not limited to financial, investment, legal, tax, business, medical, mental health, educational, psychological, or other professional guidance. Readers should conduct their own independent research and consult appropriately qualified professionals before making decisions that may affect their finances, health, business, education, legal matters, personal circumstances, or other important areas of life.

Results, outcomes, and experiences may vary significantly among individuals. Neither the author nor the publisher guarantees any specific outcomes, results, earnings, performance improvements, personal achievements, or benefits resulting from the use of information contained in this publication.

By reading, accessing, or using this publication, you acknowledge and agree that the author and publisher shall not be held liable for any direct, indirect, incidental, consequential, financial, personal, emotional, or other damages, losses, or claims arising from the use, misuse, interpretation, or application of information contained within this publication. You assume full responsibility for any actions, decisions, and outcomes resulting from the use of this material.

Image Credits and Public Domain Notice

All images, illustrations, graphics, photographs, visual references, and related materials included in this publication are believed to be in the public domain, used under applicable licenses or permissions, created by the author or publisher, or obtained from sources that clearly identify them as available for lawful use.

The author and publisher have made a good faith effort to use only visual materials that are lawfully available for use and distribution. Where applicable, images and visual materials may have been resized, cropped, edited, enhanced, stylized, modified, reformatted, or arranged for educational, informational, design, formatting, or presentation purposes.

This publication is intended for educational, informational, and illustrative purposes only. The inclusion of any image, artwork, photograph, visual reference, symbol, historical material, design, or graphic element is not intended to claim ownership over public domain materials or any third-party intellectual property rights that remain with their respective owners.

If you believe any image or visual material included in this publication has been used in error, please contact the author or publisher so the matter may be reviewed and corrected in future editions or releases if necessary.

Any factual information, specifications, historical references, values, descriptions, statistics, or related content accompanying visual materials are provided for general informational purposes only and may change over time. Readers should conduct their own independent research and consult appropriate sources or qualified professionals when making decisions based on information presented in this publication.

This publication is independently produced and is not affiliated with, endorsed by, sponsored by, or associated with any company, organization, government agency, institution, trademark holder, or third party unless specifically stated otherwise.

Table of Contents

Introduction: The Physical Side of Artificial Intelligence

Artificial intelligence often feels invisible. A person types a question, generates an image, analyzes information, or asks an AI system to complete a task, and the result appears on a screen within seconds. What is much less visible is the physical infrastructure working behind that interaction. **Artificial intelligence depends on data centers**, electricity, cooling equipment, water, computer chips, transmission systems, and other resources that exist in the physical world. As demand for AI grows, understanding this infrastructure is becoming an important part of understanding AI itself.

Why AI Depends on Physical Infrastructure

AI may be built around software, algorithms, and data, but those systems need physical machines to operate. Modern AI models can require large numbers of specialized processors working together inside data centers. These machines perform the calculations needed to train AI models and respond to users after those models have been deployed.

That computing activity requires **electricity**. Powerful processors consume energy while operating, and additional electricity is needed for networking equipment, storage systems, lighting, security, cooling, and other parts of the facility.

Heat is another important part of the equation. Computer equipment produces heat while operating. If that heat is not properly controlled, equipment can become less efficient or fail. Data centers therefore require cooling systems capable of keeping equipment within acceptable operating temperatures.

Depending on the facility, cooling may involve outside air, mechanical refrigeration, liquid cooling, evaporative systems, or combinations of different technologies. Some approaches require significant amounts of water, while others use relatively little.

This is one reason discussions about AI's environmental footprint can become complicated. There is no single amount of water or electricity that represents every AI data center.

The physical footprint also extends beyond the building.

Servers require processors, memory, storage devices, metals, plastics, circuit boards, and other materials. Those components must be manufactured and transported. Data centers must be constructed. Electricity must reach the facilities. Eventually, aging equipment must be replaced, reused, recycled, or discarded.

The environmental footprint of AI therefore involves an entire chain of physical activity rather than simply what happens when someone interacts with an AI application.

Why the Environmental Impact Is Growing

Data centers existed long before the current AI boom. They have supported websites, cloud computing, streaming services, financial systems, online shopping, business software, and countless other digital services for years.

AI is adding another major source of computing demand.

Training advanced AI models can involve enormous amounts of computation. Once those models are available, millions of individual requests can create additional demand as people and businesses use AI tools.

As companies build more computing capacity, **electricity demand from data centers can increase**. In some locations, this can create questions about whether existing power generation and transmission infrastructure can accommodate rapid growth.

Water can create similar concerns.

A data center using water-based cooling in a region with plentiful water may create a very different environmental situation from a facility using significant quantities of water in an area experiencing drought or growing competition for local supplies.

The same principle applies to emissions.

A facility receiving electricity primarily from lower-carbon energy sources can have a different carbon footprint from one relying heavily on electricity produced from fossil fuels. Backup power systems can also contribute to local emissions when generators are tested or operated.

Construction adds another layer. Large data center campuses can require substantial amounts of land, concrete, steel, electrical infrastructure, roads, transmission equipment, and other resources.

Then there is the hardware itself.

The rapid development of AI processors can encourage data center operators to replace computing equipment as newer and more efficient systems become available. Manufacturing new equipment consumes resources, while retiring older equipment raises questions about reuse and **electronic waste**.

None of these issues means that every AI application has the same environmental impact. Instead, they demonstrate why the growth of AI deserves to be examined as both a technological development and an infrastructure development.

Looking at AI Data Centers Honestly and in Context

Environmental discussions surrounding artificial intelligence can easily move toward extremes.

One extreme presents AI as an environmental disaster without adequately considering differences between facilities, technologies, locations, and energy systems. Another treats AI as purely digital and overlooks the physical resources required to support it.

A more useful approach falls between those positions.

Environmental impact depends heavily on context. Two data centers performing similar computing tasks may have substantially different footprints because they use different cooling systems, electricity sources, hardware, climates, or operating practices.

Water use provides a good example. Saying that "AI uses water" is technically useful but incomplete. The more important questions are how much water is being used, where it is being withdrawn, whether it is consumed or returned, what type of water is being used, and whether that use creates meaningful pressure on local resources.

Electricity should be examined similarly.

High electricity consumption does not automatically reveal the full environmental impact. The source of that electricity matters. So does the efficiency of the computing equipment, the efficiency of the facility, and whether new power generation or transmission infrastructure must be constructed to support additional demand.

Air quality presents another layer. A data center itself may not operate like a traditional industrial plant with continuous smokestack emissions, but fossil-fuel electricity generation and onsite backup generators can contribute to emissions associated with its operation.

There are also potential improvements worth examining.

More efficient processors can accomplish more computing work with a given amount of energy. Advanced cooling technologies may reduce certain resource requirements. Renewable and other lower-carbon energy sources can reduce emissions associated with electricity consumption. Water conservation strategies can reduce dependence on potable water. Equipment reuse and recycling can help address waste.

Some facilities may even be designed around local environmental conditions rather than applying the same cooling and energy strategy everywhere.

These developments do not erase environmental concerns. They demonstrate that the environmental footprint of AI is something that can potentially be **measured, compared, managed, and reduced**.

That distinction will guide this book.

The chapters ahead will examine how AI data centers work, why they consume water and electricity, how their operations can contribute to carbon emissions and air-quality concerns, and how their broader footprint extends into construction, land use, hardware manufacturing, waste, and surrounding communities.

The final part of the book will examine what a more sustainable approach to AI infrastructure could look like.

Last Thoughts

Artificial intelligence may appear on our phones and computers as software, but behind that software is a growing physical system of data centers, power infrastructure, cooling equipment, water systems, computer hardware, and supply chains. Understanding the environmental impact of AI therefore requires looking beyond the screen. The goal is not to assume that AI is environmentally good or bad. It is to understand **what resources AI infrastructure requires, where environmental pressures can occur, why those impacts differ, and what opportunities exist to reduce them**. That foundation will make it easier to examine the individual environmental issues surrounding AI data centers throughout the chapters ahead.

Chapter 1: How AI Data Centers Work

Artificial intelligence depends on computing infrastructure capable of processing enormous amounts of information. While traditional data centers already perform many demanding tasks, the rapid expansion of AI has introduced workloads that can require especially powerful processors and dense computing systems. Understanding what happens inside these facilities helps explain why AI can place significant demands on energy, cooling, and other resources.

What Makes an AI Data Center Different

A data center is essentially a facility designed to house and operate computing equipment at scale. Traditional data centers support everything from websites and email to cloud storage, financial transactions, streaming services, and business applications.

An **AI data center** uses much of the same basic infrastructure, but it may contain significantly more specialized computing equipment designed for artificial intelligence workloads.

One important difference is the amount of computation involved.

Many AI systems rely on models containing enormous numbers of adjustable parameters. Developing these models requires repeatedly processing large amounts of data while the system learns patterns and relationships.

This process is commonly known as **AI training**.

Training can require large groups of processors operating together for extended periods. The computers must communicate rapidly with one another, which creates additional demand for networking equipment and supporting infrastructure.

Once a model has been trained, another process begins.

AI inference occurs when a trained model responds to a request. Generating text, analyzing an image, answering a question, or producing other AI-generated content requires the model to perform calculations using its existing training.

A single request may seem insignificant compared with training an entire model. However, popular AI services can receive enormous numbers of requests. At that scale, inference can become a major source of computing demand.

This creates an important distinction when discussing environmental impact. The resources required to develop an AI model and the resources required to operate it over time are not necessarily the same.

AI facilities may also have greater concentrations of high-performance computing equipment than conventional facilities. More computing power packed into a smaller area can mean greater electricity demand and more heat that must be removed.

That brings us to the equipment inside the building.

Servers, GPUs, Cooling Systems, and Supporting Equipment

Walk into a modern data center and much of the computing equipment is organized into rows of racks. Each rack can contain servers, processors, networking hardware, storage devices, power equipment, and other components.

AI computing increasingly relies on specialized processors capable of performing many calculations simultaneously.

One of the most important is the **graphics processing unit**, commonly called a GPU.

GPUs were originally developed largely for graphics processing, but their ability to perform many mathematical operations in parallel made them useful for machine learning and modern AI.

Large AI systems may use thousands of these processors working together.

But the processors are only one part of the facility.

Data must move rapidly between machines, making high-speed networking essential. Storage systems hold information used by applications and models. Electrical equipment distributes power throughout the facility. Batteries and backup systems help keep equipment operating when normal electricity supplies are interrupted.

All of this equipment generates heat.

Cooling is therefore not optional. Maintaining appropriate temperatures is necessary for reliable operation and can account for an important portion of a facility's resource consumption.

Traditional approaches often move cooled air through server rooms. Other facilities use evaporative cooling, chilled-water systems, or combinations of different technologies.

Increasingly powerful AI hardware is also encouraging greater interest in **liquid cooling**. Instead of relying entirely on air to remove heat, liquid can be brought much closer to the processors producing it. Because liquids can transfer heat efficiently, these systems can help manage extremely dense computing environments.

The environmental consequences depend on how a cooling system is designed.

A cooling technology that reduces electricity demand could increase water requirements in certain configurations. Another system might reduce onsite water consumption while requiring more electricity. Local temperature and humidity can also influence which approach works best.

Data centers therefore involve tradeoffs between computing performance, electricity, cooling, water, reliability, and cost.

There is another important part of the facility that may remain largely unnoticed during normal operation: backup power.

Data centers are expected to operate reliably, so many facilities have generators that can provide electricity during grid outages. These generators may use diesel or other fuels. Even when emergencies are rare, generators generally need periodic testing.

This means a data center's environmental footprint cannot be determined simply by looking at the servers.

Why AI Workloads Require So Many Resources

The environmental discussion becomes easier to understand once we consider what AI hardware is actually being asked to accomplish.

Modern AI systems perform tremendous numbers of mathematical calculations. Training can involve processing large datasets repeatedly while the system adjusts itself to improve its performance.

More advanced models may require larger computing clusters, more memory, faster networking, and longer periods of operation.

The relationship is not always simple. A larger or newer AI model does not automatically consume a predictable amount more energy. Hardware efficiency, model architecture, software optimization, workload size, and facility efficiency can all influence resource requirements.

Still, one basic relationship remains important:

More computation generally requires more physical resources somewhere in the system.

Processors require electricity. Electricity becomes heat. Heat must be removed. Cooling requires equipment and may require additional electricity or water. Supporting those machines requires networking, storage, buildings, electrical systems, and backup infrastructure.

There is also a difference between **peak demand and total consumption**.

A facility can consume a large amount of electricity over an entire year while maintaining relatively steady demand. Another facility may create particularly high demand during certain periods. Both situations can present challenges for utilities, but in different ways.

Efficiency improvements can help.

Newer processors may perform more calculations for each unit of electricity consumed. Software can be optimized. Cooling systems can become more efficient. Operators can improve how computing workloads are distributed.

However, efficiency does not automatically guarantee that total resource consumption will fall.

If AI becomes cheaper and more efficient, businesses may simply use much more of it. Millions of additional users, applications, automated systems, and AI agents could increase total computing demand even as individual calculations become more efficient.

This is one of the central challenges in evaluating the future environmental footprint of AI.

The question is not simply whether AI computers become more efficient. It is whether efficiency improvements happen quickly enough to offset the growth in the total amount of computing being performed.

Understanding that distinction prevents the environmental discussion from becoming overly simplistic.

AI data centers are not mysterious machines consuming resources for no reason. They are large computing facilities converting electricity into enormous amounts of computational work. The environmental question is how efficiently that work can be performed and what resources are required to support it.

Last Thoughts

Understanding how AI data centers work provides the foundation for understanding their environmental impact. AI workloads can require specialized processors, extensive networking, reliable power, and sophisticated cooling systems operating together at enormous scale. Greater computing demand can translate into greater resource demand, although the actual footprint depends heavily on hardware, software, facility design, location, and energy sources. One resource deserves particular attention because it is often less visible than electricity: water. In the next chapter, we will examine why some data centers consume water, how cooling systems influence that consumption, and why the local availability of water can matter just as much as the amount being used.

Chapter 2: Water Consumption and Cooling

Water has become one of the most discussed environmental issues surrounding AI data centers. Powerful computing equipment generates substantial heat, and that heat must be continuously managed to keep servers operating safely and efficiently. Some cooling approaches use very little water onsite, while others can consume significant amounts. Understanding this difference is important because simply saying that AI "uses water" does not explain where the water goes, why it is needed, or how much pressure that use may place on a particular community.

Why Data Centers Use Water

The computers inside a data center convert much of the electricity they consume into heat. As more high-performance processors are placed inside a facility, removing that heat becomes increasingly important.

Water can be useful because it is highly effective at absorbing and transferring heat.

One common approach involves **evaporative cooling**. In these systems, water helps remove heat as some of it evaporates into the atmosphere. Evaporation can reduce the amount of electricity required for mechanical cooling under certain conditions, but the water that evaporates is no longer immediately available to the local water system.

Other facilities may use chilled-water systems that circulate water through cooling equipment. Some systems operate primarily as closed loops, meaning water is repeatedly circulated rather than constantly replaced.

Even these systems may require additional water for cooling towers or other parts of the cooling process.

Not every data center relies heavily on water.

Facilities can also use air cooling, refrigerant-based systems, closed-loop liquid systems, or combinations of several technologies. Climate plays an important role. A facility located in a cool region may be able to use outside air during parts of the year, while a facility in a hotter environment may require more intensive cooling.

There is also an indirect connection between data centers and water.

Electricity generation itself can require water. Certain power plants use water for cooling and other operations. This means a data center may have an **indirect water footprint** associated with the electricity it purchases, even when the facility itself consumes relatively little water.

The complete picture therefore includes both the water used at the data center and water potentially used elsewhere to support its electricity demand.

Cooling Systems and Water Consumption

One of the difficulties with comparing data center water use is that cooling systems can be designed very differently.

Some operators measure performance using **water usage effectiveness**, often abbreviated WUE. This metric can help describe how much water a facility uses in relation to the computing energy being consumed.

A lower number generally indicates that less water is being used for the amount of computing activity performed.

However, a single number still does not tell the entire story.

The type of water matters.

Some facilities may rely on drinking-quality municipal water, while others can use reclaimed or recycled water that would otherwise have fewer competing uses. A facility that reduces its dependence on potable water may place less pressure on drinking-water supplies even if cooling still requires substantial quantities of water.

The timing of water consumption also matters.

Using water during a wet season may create different pressures than consuming the same amount during a drought or period of extreme heat. Unfortunately, extreme heat is also when cooling requirements can become greater.

This can create a difficult tradeoff.

A cooling system may use additional water to reduce electricity consumption. Another design may conserve water but require more electricity to operate mechanical cooling equipment.

Neither approach is automatically environmentally superior in every location.

In a water-stressed region, reducing water consumption might be the higher priority. In an area with abundant reclaimed water but a carbon-intensive electricity supply, reducing electricity consumption could produce different environmental benefits.

New cooling technologies may help change this balance.

Direct-to-chip liquid cooling can transfer heat away from powerful processors more efficiently than traditional room-scale air cooling in certain applications. Other approaches attempt to operate closed systems that minimize ongoing water consumption.

Data center operators can also adjust operating temperatures, improve airflow, reuse water, and design facilities around local climate conditions.

The goal is not necessarily to eliminate cooling resources entirely. Computing equipment will continue producing heat. The challenge is to remove that heat using the smallest reasonable combination of water, electricity, and other resources.

Local Water Supplies and Community Concerns

Total water consumption becomes especially important when it is considered in a local context.

A large data center may consume an amount of water that is manageable for one community but significant for another.

This is why **water stress** matters.

Water stress occurs when demand for available water begins placing pressure on the quantity or quality of supplies. Population growth, agriculture, industry, drought, climate conditions, and other users can all contribute.

Adding a large data center to an already stressed system can create concerns about competition for water.

Residents may reasonably ask whether new industrial demand could affect household supplies, groundwater levels, future development, or water prices. Farmers and other businesses may have similar concerns.

These questions become more complicated when multiple data centers are constructed in the same region.

One facility may represent a relatively small portion of local demand. Several large facilities operating together can create a much larger cumulative impact.

Transparency therefore becomes important.

Communities need enough information to understand how much water a proposed facility expects to use, where that water will come from, whether potable or reclaimed water will be used, and how consumption could change during hot or dry periods.

Data center developers can also consider local conditions before deciding where and how facilities should be built.

A cooling strategy appropriate for a water-rich region may not make sense in an arid one. Similarly, locating water-intensive facilities in areas already facing shortages can create environmental and community conflicts that might have been reduced through different designs or locations.

There are also opportunities for improvement.

Facilities can use reclaimed wastewater where appropriate, reduce evaporation, capture and reuse water, adopt less water-intensive cooling technologies, and monitor consumption more carefully.

The important point is that **water consumption should be evaluated locally**, not simply globally.

A gallon of water does not carry the same environmental significance everywhere. Its importance depends on where it comes from, what competing demands exist, when it is consumed, and whether it can be replaced or reused.

That context is essential when evaluating claims about AI and water.

Last Thoughts

AI data centers can require water because powerful computing equipment generates heat that must be removed, but the amount and significance of that water use vary considerably. Cooling technology, climate, facility design, water source, electricity generation, and local availability all influence the final footprint. This means the environmental question is not simply whether AI data centers use water. The more useful question is **how much water they consume, where that water comes from, and what that consumption means for the surrounding community**. Water is only one part of the resource equation, however. The next major issue is electricity, which connects AI data centers to power plants, transmission infrastructure, and the wider electrical grid.

Chapter 3: Electricity Demand and the Power Grid

Electricity is one of the most important resources behind artificial intelligence. Every calculation performed by an AI system ultimately depends on electrical power flowing through processors, networking equipment, storage systems, and cooling infrastructure. As AI data centers grow larger and more numerous, their electricity requirements are becoming an increasingly important part of the environmental discussion. The issue is not only how much electricity these facilities consume, but also whether power grids can support their growth and how that electricity is generated.

Why AI Requires So Much Electricity

AI systems perform enormous numbers of mathematical calculations. Training a large model can require many specialized processors operating continuously for extended periods, while everyday use requires additional computing whenever users interact with the model.

Each processor consumes electricity while operating.

When thousands of processors are installed together, the combined demand can become substantial. Electricity is also required for networking equipment, storage systems, pumps, fans, cooling equipment, security systems, and other infrastructure necessary to keep the facility operating.

This creates **computing power density**, meaning a large amount of computing equipment and electrical demand can be concentrated within a relatively small physical area.

AI workloads can make this particularly challenging.

A conventional server rack may operate at a lower power level than a rack packed with high-performance AI processors. As more powerful hardware is installed, data center designers must ensure that enough electricity can safely reach the equipment while also managing the additional heat it produces.

There is also a difference between training and everyday AI use.

Training may create extremely intensive computing workloads for a limited period. Once an AI model is available, however, inference can continue around the clock as people and businesses use it.

A popular AI system serving millions of users can therefore create substantial ongoing electricity demand.

Efficiency improvements can reduce the electricity required for individual calculations. Newer processors can perform more work per unit of energy, while better software can reduce unnecessary computation.

But total electricity consumption can still rise if AI use grows faster than efficiency improves.

This means the environmental challenge is influenced by both **efficiency and scale**.

An AI system that becomes twice as efficient may still consume more total electricity if its usage increases several times over.

Data Centers and Growing Pressure on Power Grids

Electricity does not simply appear at a data center. It must be generated, transmitted over power lines, distributed through local infrastructure, and delivered reliably to the facility.

Rapid data center development can therefore create challenges for the **electrical grid**.

Power grids were generally built around expected levels of residential, commercial, and industrial demand. When a very large data center is proposed, utilities may suddenly need to accommodate a major new source of electricity consumption.

In some areas, existing infrastructure may be sufficient.

In others, additional substations, transmission lines, transformers, power generation, or other equipment may be necessary.

These projects take time.

A data center can sometimes be constructed faster than major electrical infrastructure can be planned, approved, and built. This can create delays and force utilities, developers, regulators, and communities to decide how new demand should be accommodated.

There are also questions about who pays for the required upgrades.

If a new data center requires major investments in transmission or generation capacity, communities may want to know whether those costs will be paid primarily by the data center operator or spread across other electricity customers.

Reliability is another concern.

Data centers often operate continuously and require dependable electricity. Utilities must ensure that adding large new customers does not reduce their ability to provide reliable power to homes, hospitals, businesses, schools, and other existing users.

However, large data centers can also become participants in grid management.

Some facilities may adjust certain computing workloads to periods when electricity is more available. Batteries can provide temporary power or help manage demand. In some circumstances, operators may coordinate with utilities to reduce electricity consumption during periods of extreme grid stress.

This practice is part of a broader concept known as **demand flexibility**.

Not every AI workload can easily be moved or delayed. Real-time services must remain responsive. But certain training jobs and other computing activities may offer more flexibility.

If managed effectively, flexibility could allow some data centers to better match their electricity use with periods when the grid has available capacity.

Where the Electricity Comes From Matters

Electricity consumption alone does not reveal the full environmental footprint of an AI data center.

The source of the electricity is equally important.

A facility powered by an electricity system heavily dependent on coal or natural gas may be associated with greater carbon emissions than a similar facility drawing from a grid with large amounts of nuclear, hydroelectric, wind, solar, or other lower-carbon generation.

This is why **electricity mix** matters when evaluating AI's environmental impact.

Data centers do not always receive electricity directly from a single power plant. Most connect to regional grids where electricity from multiple sources is combined.

Companies may purchase renewable energy or enter agreements intended to support new clean-energy projects. These arrangements can help increase lower-carbon electricity generation, but they do not necessarily mean that a facility physically receives renewable electricity every hour it operates.

Timing matters because wind and solar generation vary.

A facility may consume electricity continuously while renewable generation changes throughout the day. When renewable production is unavailable, other sources may supply the grid.

For this reason, some sustainability efforts increasingly focus not only on how much clean electricity is purchased over a year, but also on whether lower-carbon electricity is available during the same hours that the data center is consuming power.

AI growth could also influence the development of new energy resources.

In some regions, utilities may build additional renewable generation and battery storage. Other areas may extend the operation of existing power plants or construct new natural gas generation to meet growing demand. Nuclear power and other technologies may also become part of the discussion.

Each approach creates different environmental tradeoffs.

Renewable energy can reduce operational carbon emissions but requires land, materials, transmission infrastructure, and storage or other resources to manage variability. Fossil-fuel generation can provide dependable power but produces greenhouse gas emissions and potentially other air pollutants.

No electricity source is entirely without environmental consequences.

The important question is what combination of resources can provide reliable electricity while minimizing emissions and other environmental pressures.

For AI data centers, this makes location particularly important. Building the same facility in two different regions can result in different environmental footprints simply because the surrounding electrical systems are different.

Last Thoughts

The electricity required to operate AI data centers connects artificial intelligence directly to the larger energy system. Growing computing demand can require additional generation, transmission lines, substations, and other grid infrastructure, particularly in regions experiencing rapid data center development. At the same time, the environmental consequences depend heavily on **how that electricity is produced**. Greater efficiency, cleaner electricity, energy storage, and flexible computing workloads can reduce some of the pressure, but rapid growth in AI usage may continue pushing total electricity demand higher. Electricity also leads directly to another environmental concern: the carbon emissions and air pollutants associated with producing power and maintaining reliable backup systems.

Chapter 4: Carbon Emissions and Air Quality

AI data centers do not all produce the same level of emissions. Much depends on where their electricity comes from, how efficiently the facilities operate, and what backup power systems they use. Some environmental effects occur far from the data center at the power plants supplying its electricity, while others can occur directly at the facility. Understanding this distinction is important when evaluating both the carbon footprint of AI and its potential effects on local air quality.

Understanding the Carbon Footprint of AI

The **carbon footprint of AI** includes greenhouse gas emissions associated with the computing infrastructure required to develop and operate AI systems.

A major portion of this footprint can come from electricity generation.

When electricity is produced using fossil fuels such as coal or natural gas, carbon dioxide and other emissions are released during power generation. A data center drawing heavily from a fossil-fuel-dependent grid can therefore be associated with significant emissions even though those emissions may occur at power plants located somewhere else.

Facilities connected to electrical systems with larger amounts of lower-carbon generation can have a different operational footprint.

Efficiency also matters.

More efficient processors can perform greater amounts of computational work using the same amount of electricity. Efficient cooling, power distribution, and facility design can further reduce unnecessary energy consumption.

However, improvements in efficiency must be considered alongside the rapid expansion of AI.

If each AI task requires less electricity but the total number of AI tasks increases dramatically, overall energy consumption and associated emissions can still rise.

There are also emissions beyond everyday electricity use.

Constructing data centers requires concrete, steel, glass, electrical equipment, and other materials. Manufacturing servers and advanced computer chips requires energy and industrial processes. Equipment must also be transported between manufacturing facilities, distribution centers, and data center sites.

These activities contribute to **embodied carbon**, which refers to emissions associated with producing, transporting, constructing, and eventually disposing of physical materials and equipment.

This means an AI system's carbon footprint extends beyond the electricity consumed while someone is actually using it.

Backup Generators and Local Air Pollution

Data centers are designed to operate reliably. Even a relatively short power interruption can disrupt services used by businesses, governments, consumers, and other organizations.

For this reason, facilities commonly maintain backup power systems.

Traditionally, these have often included **diesel generators** capable of supplying electricity when normal grid power is unavailable.

Generators may also be operated periodically for testing and maintenance. Operators need to know that the equipment will function when an emergency occurs.

Burning diesel fuel produces air pollutants.

Depending on the engine and pollution-control equipment, emissions can include nitrogen oxides, particulate matter, carbon monoxide, and other pollutants. These emissions can contribute to local air-quality concerns, particularly when many generators are concentrated at a large data center campus.

Location becomes especially important.

A facility located far from densely populated areas may create a different exposure situation from one located near homes, schools, or communities already affected by other sources of air pollution.

The frequency of generator operation matters as well.

Backup generators that operate only occasionally during emergencies have a different impact from generators that run more frequently because of grid conditions or other operational needs.

This is why simply counting the number of generators at a facility does not provide a complete picture.

Communities and regulators may consider the type of fuel being used, generator capacity, expected operating hours, emissions controls, testing schedules, and nearby populations when evaluating potential air-quality effects.

Alternative backup technologies could reduce some of these concerns.

Large battery systems can provide electricity during short interruptions and may reduce the need to immediately start generators. Other technologies and cleaner fuels are also being explored.

However, providing reliable backup power for a large data center can be challenging. Batteries capable of supporting an enormous computing facility for long periods can require significant capacity.

Backup power therefore remains another area where reliability and environmental considerations must be balanced.

Direct and Indirect Emissions

One of the easiest ways to misunderstand the environmental footprint of a data center is to look only at emissions physically produced at the facility.

Direct emissions come from sources controlled or operated at the site. Fuel burned by backup generators is one example.

Indirect emissions occur elsewhere because of activities required to operate the facility.

Electricity provides the clearest example.

A data center may purchase electricity from the grid without burning fossil fuels inside the building. However, if power plants burn coal or natural gas to produce some of that electricity, emissions are still associated with the facility's energy consumption.

The supply chain adds another layer.

Manufacturing advanced processors requires highly specialized factories, large amounts of energy, water, chemicals, and raw materials. Servers require metals, circuit boards, memory, storage devices, and other components produced through global supply chains.

Constructing the data center itself also creates emissions before the first AI workload begins operating.

These differences explain why environmental assessments can produce very different numbers depending on what is being measured.

One calculation might consider only electricity used by computing equipment. Another might include cooling and other facility operations. A broader assessment could include electricity generation, hardware manufacturing, construction, transportation, and equipment disposal.

None of these approaches necessarily answers every environmental question.

What matters is understanding the boundaries of the measurement.

When someone claims that an AI system produces a particular amount of carbon emissions, it is useful to ask what has actually been included in that calculation.

This is especially important as AI infrastructure expands.

The environmental footprint is not limited to the moment a user submits a prompt. It includes portions of a much larger system required to build, power, cool, maintain, and eventually replace the equipment making that interaction possible.

At the same time, recognizing these indirect effects should not lead to the assumption that every AI application carries an identical environmental cost.

Different models require different amounts of computation. Hardware efficiency varies. Electricity sources vary by location and time. Data centers use different cooling systems and operating practices.

Understanding these differences allows environmental impacts to be evaluated more accurately rather than reduced to a single universal number.

Last Thoughts

Carbon emissions and air quality reveal how the environmental footprint of AI extends beyond the walls of a data center. Electricity generation can create emissions far from the facility, while backup generators can contribute to pollution closer to surrounding communities. Construction and hardware manufacturing add another layer through embodied carbon and global supply chains. Looking at **both direct and indirect emissions** provides a more complete understanding of the environmental cost of AI infrastructure. But emissions are still only part of the picture. Building and continuously upgrading large data centers also requires land, physical materials, computing hardware, and eventually decisions about what happens to equipment when it reaches the end of its useful life.

Chapter 5: Land, Hardware, Waste, and Local Communities

The environmental footprint of AI data centers extends beyond water, electricity, and emissions. These facilities must be constructed somewhere, filled with enormous amounts of computing equipment, connected to supporting infrastructure, and continually maintained as technology changes. As data center development accelerates, questions about land use, manufacturing, electronic waste, and effects on surrounding communities are becoming increasingly important.

Construction, Land Use, and Supporting Infrastructure

Large data centers can occupy substantial areas of land. A single building may be only one part of a much larger campus containing electrical substations, cooling equipment, backup generators, water infrastructure, security areas, parking, roads, and other supporting systems.

The physical footprint can grow further when multiple facilities are developed together.

This creates **land-use considerations** that vary significantly depending on where a facility is built.

Constructing a data center on previously developed industrial property may have different environmental consequences from clearing forests, farmland, or other undeveloped land. Development can alter drainage patterns, remove vegetation, disturb habitats, and increase the amount of land covered by buildings and pavement.

Construction itself also requires significant quantities of materials.

Concrete and steel are commonly used in large buildings and supporting infrastructure. Manufacturing these materials requires energy and contributes to emissions before the data center even begins operating.

The surrounding electrical system may also need to expand.

New transmission lines, substations, transformers, and power-generation resources can require additional land. Water and wastewater infrastructure may need upgrades as well.

This means the physical footprint associated with a data center can extend beyond the boundaries of the property.

Location decisions therefore matter.

Building near existing electrical, water, transportation, and communications infrastructure can sometimes reduce the amount of new infrastructure required. Thoughtful site planning can also help reduce disruption to sensitive land and surrounding communities.

As AI infrastructure expands, evaluating the environmental effects of construction becomes an important part of understanding its overall footprint.

Chips, Servers, Electronic Waste, and the Supply Chain

Inside every AI data center are thousands of physical components.

Processors, memory, storage devices, circuit boards, networking equipment, cables, batteries, cooling systems, and power equipment must all be manufactured before an AI system can operate.

These products require raw materials.

Semiconductor manufacturing uses silicon and numerous metals, chemicals, gases, and other specialized materials. Servers and electrical systems can contain copper, aluminum, steel, plastics, and a variety of additional materials.

Extracting and processing these resources creates environmental impacts of its own.

Mining can disturb land and require significant quantities of energy and water. Refining metals requires additional energy. Semiconductor manufacturing can also require substantial amounts of electricity and highly purified water.

The result is a **hardware supply chain** extending around the world.

Components may travel through several countries during manufacturing before eventually reaching a data center. Transportation adds another layer to the environmental footprint.

Eventually, equipment must also be replaced.

AI hardware is developing rapidly. New processors can provide greater performance and improved energy efficiency, creating financial and operational incentives to upgrade older systems.

This raises concerns about **electronic waste**, commonly called e-waste.

Retired servers and other equipment contain materials that may still have value. Functional equipment can sometimes be reused for less demanding computing tasks. Components can also be refurbished, resold, or recycled.

Recycling can recover metals and other useful materials, reducing some demand for newly extracted resources.

However, electronics are complex products, and recovering every material economically is difficult. Improper disposal can also create environmental problems when hazardous substances are released into soil, water, or air.

Extending equipment life where practical can help reduce waste. Designing hardware for repair, reuse, and recycling can also improve what happens at the end of its useful life.

The environmental impact of AI hardware therefore begins long before equipment enters a data center and continues after it leaves.

How Data Center Growth Can Affect Communities

Environmental impacts are ultimately experienced somewhere.

Data centers are built near communities whose residents may experience both benefits and concerns associated with development.

Large projects can generate construction activity, tax revenue, infrastructure investment, and permanent employment. They may also attract additional technology development to a region.

At the same time, residents may have questions about **community impact**.

Water consumption can become controversial in places where supplies are already under pressure. Large electricity requirements can raise questions about grid reliability, new power plants, transmission lines, and electricity costs.

Backup generators can create concerns about local air pollution. Cooling equipment and generators can also produce noise, particularly when facilities operate around the clock.

Land development can change the character of an area as large industrial buildings replace open land, forests, or agricultural property.

Traffic may increase during construction. New electrical infrastructure may require additional transmission corridors. Communities may also question whether the economic benefits of development are proportional to the resources being used.

These concerns do not mean that every data center negatively affects its neighbors.

The effects depend on the facility, location, regulations, infrastructure, and relationship between developers and the surrounding community.

Transparency can make a significant difference.

Residents are better able to evaluate proposed developments when information about expected water consumption, electricity requirements, generator use, land development, and infrastructure needs is available.

Community involvement can also help identify concerns before construction begins.

For example, developers may be able to modify site plans, improve landscaping, reduce noise, use reclaimed water, locate generators farther from residential areas, or fund infrastructure improvements.

The rapid growth of AI makes these conversations increasingly important.

Data centers may serve users around the world, but their physical environmental effects are concentrated in particular places. The people living near those facilities can experience consequences that distant AI users rarely see.

Understanding that relationship helps connect the seemingly invisible world of artificial intelligence with the physical communities supporting it.

Last Thoughts

The environmental footprint of AI data centers extends throughout their physical life cycle. Land must be developed, buildings constructed, infrastructure installed, computer hardware manufactured, and aging equipment eventually reused, recycled, or discarded. These activities can affect ecosystems, natural resources, supply chains, and the communities hosting data center development. Recognizing these impacts does not mean that AI infrastructure cannot continue growing. It means that **how and where that growth occurs matters**. The final chapter will examine how cleaner energy, better cooling, improved efficiency, water conservation, and other strategies could reduce some of these environmental pressures while allowing AI infrastructure to continue evolving.

Chapter 6: Can AI Data Centers Become More Sustainable?

The environmental challenges associated with AI data centers are significant, but they are not necessarily fixed. The way data centers are powered, cooled, designed, and operated can change. Improvements in computing hardware can also allow more AI work to be performed with fewer resources. The question is not whether AI infrastructure can operate without any environmental footprint, but how much that footprint can realistically be reduced as demand for artificial intelligence continues to grow.

Cleaner Energy, Efficient Computing, and Better Cooling

Electricity is central to the environmental footprint of AI, which makes cleaner power one of the most important opportunities for improvement.

Data center operators can support electricity from wind, solar, hydroelectric, nuclear, geothermal, and other lower-carbon sources. The appropriate combination will depend on location, grid conditions, reliability requirements, and available resources.

The challenge is maintaining dependable electricity around the clock.

Wind and solar generation can vary with weather and time of day. Batteries can store electricity for later use, but large data centers can require enormous amounts of power. Other generation sources and grid connections may therefore remain necessary.

Another strategy is **carbon-aware computing**.

Certain computing tasks may be scheduled for periods when lower-carbon electricity is more readily available. Some workloads might even be shifted between data centers in different regions when practical.

Not every workload offers this flexibility. Users expect many AI services to respond immediately. Large training projects and other less time-sensitive computing tasks, however, may provide more opportunities for scheduling.

Hardware efficiency is equally important.

New processors can perform greater amounts of computational work for a given amount of electricity. Software developers can also design models and applications that require fewer calculations to accomplish useful tasks.

This can reduce the energy required for individual AI operations.

Cooling technology offers another opportunity.

High-density AI processors can produce large amounts of heat in relatively small spaces. More efficient cooling systems can remove that heat while reducing the electricity or water required to maintain safe operating temperatures.

Advanced liquid-cooling systems are particularly important for increasingly powerful computing hardware. Rather than cooling an entire room primarily with cold air, these systems can move heat directly away from the equipment producing it.

There is also growing interest in **waste heat reuse**.

Instead of simply releasing heat from data centers into the surrounding environment, some facilities may be able to redirect it for nearby buildings, industrial processes, or district heating systems.

The practicality of heat reuse depends heavily on location. A data center must be close enough to a suitable user of that heat, and additional infrastructure is required to transport it.

Still, the concept demonstrates how resources traditionally considered waste can sometimes become useful.

Reducing Water Use, Emissions, and Waste

Water conservation can take several forms.

Facilities can select cooling systems appropriate for local climate conditions, use reclaimed water instead of drinking-quality water where practical, improve water recycling, and reduce unnecessary evaporation.

Some facilities may prioritize **water-positive strategies**, which attempt to restore or replenish water resources in addition to reducing consumption.

These efforts should still be evaluated carefully.

Supporting a water restoration project somewhere else does not necessarily eliminate the effects of consuming water in a community experiencing local shortages. Reducing pressure on the actual watershed supporting a facility can be particularly important.

Emissions can also be addressed from several directions.

Cleaner electricity can reduce emissions associated with normal operations. More efficient equipment can reduce total electricity requirements. Batteries and alternative backup systems may reduce dependence on diesel generators for shorter power interruptions.

Better pollution-control equipment can further reduce emissions when generators must still be used.

Construction presents additional opportunities.

Lower-carbon building materials, efficient facility designs, careful site selection, and reuse of previously developed land can reduce some of the environmental impacts associated with new construction.

Hardware deserves similar attention.

Extending the useful life of servers can reduce the frequency with which equipment must be replaced. Older processors that are no longer efficient enough for demanding AI workloads may still be useful for less intensive computing.

Equipment can also be refurbished and resold.

When hardware truly reaches the end of its useful life, responsible recycling can recover valuable materials and reduce the amount entering landfills.

This approach contributes to a **circular economy**, where products and materials remain useful for as long as reasonably possible instead of following a simple manufacture, use, and disposal cycle.

Manufacturers also have a role.

Designing equipment that is easier to repair, upgrade, disassemble, and recycle can make resource recovery more practical.

No individual strategy solves the entire environmental problem.

Cleaner electricity does not eliminate water consumption. Water-efficient cooling does not eliminate hardware manufacturing. Recycling servers does not eliminate electricity demand.

Sustainability therefore requires addressing several parts of the system simultaneously.

The Tradeoffs and Future of Sustainable AI Infrastructure

One of the most important lessons from examining AI data centers is that environmental decisions frequently involve tradeoffs.

A cooling system that reduces water consumption may require additional electricity.

A facility built near abundant renewable energy may require new transmission infrastructure.

Replacing older processors with more efficient equipment may reduce operational electricity consumption while creating additional manufacturing impacts and electronic waste.

Even efficiency improvements can produce unexpected results.

If AI becomes dramatically cheaper and more efficient, its use may expand even faster. More businesses may adopt AI, more applications may include it, and automated systems may perform far greater numbers of computations.

This possibility is related to the **rebound effect**, where improvements in efficiency can encourage greater consumption and partially offset the resources saved by those improvements.

That does not make efficiency unimportant.

It means efficiency must be considered alongside total demand.

The future environmental footprint of AI will therefore depend on more than technological improvements. It will also depend on how quickly AI demand grows, where new data centers are constructed, what energy systems support them, and what environmental standards guide their development.

Measurement and transparency will matter as well.

Companies, governments, researchers, and communities need reliable information about electricity consumption, water use, emissions, and other environmental effects if they are going to determine whether improvements are actually occurring.

Communities hosting data centers will remain an important part of this discussion.

Environmental sustainability cannot be measured only through global carbon numbers. Local water availability, air quality, land development, noise, infrastructure, and electricity systems also matter.

There is unlikely to be one perfect model for a sustainable AI data center.

A facility in a cool, water-rich region may make different environmental decisions from one in a hot, dry region. A facility connected to a low-carbon electrical grid may have different priorities from one operating in an area dependent on fossil fuels.

The most sustainable approach is therefore likely to be one that considers local conditions rather than applying the same solution everywhere.

Last Thoughts

AI data centers will continue to have a physical environmental footprint as long as artificial intelligence requires electricity, computing hardware, cooling, buildings, and supporting infrastructure. The opportunity is to make that footprint smaller and more responsible. Cleaner electricity, efficient processors, better cooling, water conservation, heat reuse, responsible construction, longer equipment life, and recycling can all contribute. At the same time, rapid growth in AI could offset some of those improvements by increasing total demand. The future environmental impact of AI will ultimately depend not only on **how efficient individual data centers become, but also on how much AI infrastructure society builds and how responsibly that infrastructure is developed**.

Last Thoughts: Understanding AI's Environmental Footprint

Artificial intelligence is often discussed as though it exists entirely in a digital world. In reality, every AI interaction depends on physical infrastructure somewhere. Data centers contain processors that consume electricity, cooling systems that remove heat, electrical equipment that keeps machines operating, and networks that connect those machines with users around the world. Once this physical side of AI becomes visible, its environmental impact becomes easier to understand.

Throughout this book, we have seen that there is no single environmental footprint that applies to every AI data center.

Location matters.

Cooling technology matters.

The source of electricity matters.

The efficiency of the computing equipment matters.

The availability of local water matters.

Even the type of AI workload being performed can influence the amount of computing resources required.

This is why simple statements about AI being either environmentally harmful or environmentally sustainable can miss important details.

A data center located in a region with abundant lower-carbon electricity and carefully managed water resources may create a very different environmental footprint from a similar facility operating in an area facing water shortages or relying heavily on fossil-fuel electricity.

The same is true for individual AI systems.

Different models require different amounts of computation. Different processors operate at different levels of efficiency. Training, inference, and other computing activities can also create different resource demands.

The environmental conversation therefore needs context.

Water consumption should be considered alongside local water availability.

Electricity consumption should be considered alongside the sources generating that electricity.

Carbon emissions should include both the operation of facilities and the larger infrastructure supporting them.

Air-quality concerns should consider power generation, backup generators, location, and nearby communities.

Hardware should be considered throughout its entire life cycle, from raw material extraction and manufacturing to reuse, recycling, and eventual disposal.

And land use should include not only the data center building but also the supporting infrastructure that may be required around it.

None of this means that artificial intelligence must stop developing.

It means that the physical infrastructure supporting that development deserves attention.

There are meaningful opportunities to reduce environmental pressures. More efficient computing equipment can perform greater amounts of work with less energy. Improved cooling technologies can reduce resource requirements. Cleaner electricity can lower emissions. Reclaimed water can reduce pressure on drinking-water supplies. Better hardware management can extend equipment life and reduce waste.

Data center developers can also make better decisions about where facilities are constructed and how those facilities interact with surrounding communities.

But technological improvements alone may not determine the outcome.

AI usage is growing quickly. If the total amount of computing expands faster than efficiency improves, overall electricity, water, hardware, and infrastructure requirements could continue increasing.

That creates one of the most important questions surrounding the future of AI:

Can the environmental efficiency of AI infrastructure improve quickly enough to keep pace with the enormous growth in demand?

The answer will depend on decisions being made now and in the years ahead.

Technology companies will influence how efficiently AI systems are designed. Data center operators will influence how facilities are powered and cooled. Utilities will influence how additional electricity demand is supplied. Governments and regulators will influence where infrastructure can be constructed and what environmental requirements must be met.

Communities will also have a role.

The benefits of AI may be distributed around the world, but many of its environmental effects are experienced locally. Communities hosting large data centers have legitimate reasons to understand how those facilities may affect water supplies, electricity systems, air quality, land, infrastructure, and future development.

Greater transparency can help make those conversations more productive.

The goal should not be to treat AI as an environmental villain or to ignore its physical footprint because of its technological benefits.

The more useful approach is to recognize both realities.

Artificial intelligence can provide valuable tools, improve productivity, support scientific research, assist businesses, and create new technological possibilities.

At the same time, those capabilities require physical resources.

Understanding that connection allows society to ask better questions about how AI infrastructure should grow.

The environmental future of artificial intelligence is not predetermined. It will be shaped by choices about energy, water, computing efficiency, construction, hardware, waste, location, and responsible development.

As AI becomes increasingly integrated into everyday life, understanding those choices will become just as important as understanding the technology itself.

About the Author

Roggie "Raj" Clark is an entrepreneur and a 10-year marketing professional with a proven track record in e-commerce and digital business growth. Having built and managed successful online stores with thousands of sales and consulted for numerous marketing clients, Roggie has mastered the intricacies of online marketing, branding, and consumer behavior. He has also written several popular books on digital marketing, SEO (search engine optimization), and programming (HTML, CSS, and JavaScript).

As a former marketing manager at a fintech company—a role he secured through his own marketing and financial expertise—Roggie gained firsthand experience in financial strategy and wealth-building. This journey inspired him to share insights with amateur investors, helping them save money, make smarter financial decisions, and build long-term wealth. Raj currently lives in Maryland with his sister and niece.

www.ingramcontent.com/pod-product-compliance
Lightning Source LLC
LaVergne TN
LVHW050747061126
851857LV00013B/1030
9781088264126